Understanding your
Senses

Making sense of this subject were:

Rebecca Treays who wrote the words
(with the help of **Gillian Doherty** & **Emma Danes**)
Christyan Fox who drew the pictures
Professor Nicholas Mackintosh, the sense

D1306640

Martin Aggett who did the designs

INTRODUCTION

Your senses let you know what is going on in the outside world and to your own body. Without them, you would be completely cut off from everything around you. You wouldn't even know whether your arms were folded or your legs crossed. You have five main senses: sight, hearing, taste, smell and feeling, or touch. The parts of your body which can sense things are called sense organs.

CONTENTS

You need your senses to do all the things shown in these pictures.

See

Know the position of parts of your body

Balance

Touch or feel

GETTING THE PICTURE

Sight is the sense which gives you most information about the world. But if you were blindfolded, you'd be surprised how quickly your other senses could help you find out about what is around you.

Smell

It's a vase...
made in 1927 by
a left-handed
potter.

Err...
Yes.

Hands feel objects around you.

What was that?

Shhhh...

Ears tell you where people are.

North, Northwest,
two paces...

Smell leads you to food.

mmm...chicken, free
range, corn fed,
roasted on 350°F
for one hour
forty minutes.

Forty five.

Taste tells you it's good to eat.

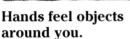

Taste

Hear

SIXTH SENSE

Sometimes you can have a vague "feeling" that something is happening, without seeming to see, hear, taste, smell or feel it. People often call this their "sixth sense". In fact, your senses have probably picked up something so tiny that you weren't even aware of it, such as a tiny breath of wind.

Hello,
I'm Norman the
Neuron.

You will find out how important neurons, or nerve cells, are on page 4.

GETTING INFORMATION

The parts of your sense organs that can tell what is happening are called receptors. Receptors convert information into electrical pulses which are sent to your brain along nerve cells. Your brain analyzes the information and makes you aware of what is going on. It may then send instructions back to parts of your body, making them act upon this information.

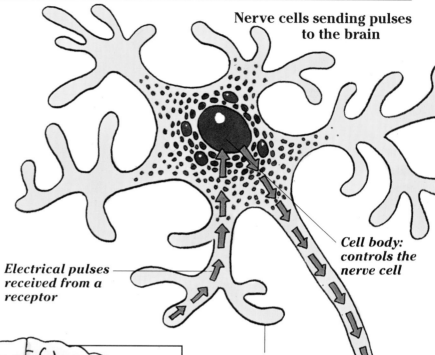

Nerve cells sending pulses to the brain

Electrical pulses received from a receptor

Cell body: controls the nerve cell

Dendrite: short tentacle which carries pulses to the cell body

Axon: long tentacle which carries pulses away from the cell body

NERVE CELLS

Nerve cells, or neurons, carry pulses of electricity from receptors to your brain. Each neuron is made up of a cell body, an axon and up to several hundred dendrites.

When a pulse reaches the end of an axon, chemicals are released. These spread to the nearest dendrite and spark off a pulse in the next neuron. Pulses are passed from one nerve cell to the next, until the information reaches the brain.

BRAIN MAP

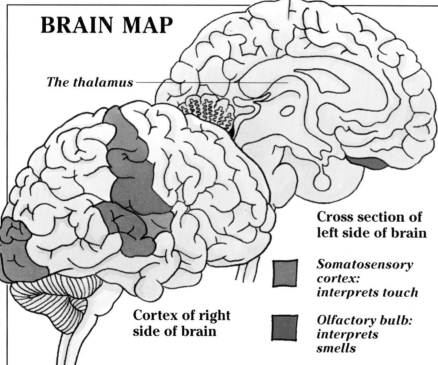

The thalamus

Cortex of right side of brain

Cross section of left side of brain

Somatosensory cortex: interprets touch

Olfactory bulb: interprets smells

Auditory cortex: interprets sounds

Visual (or striate) cortex: interprets sights

Gustatory cortex: interprets tastes

Information from your senses is sent to a part of your brain called the cortex. Different areas of the cortex deal with a different sense. Signals are directed to the correct area by a part of your brain called the thalamus.

DIFFERENT RECEPTORS

The receptors in your different sense organs are designed to detect and respond to different things. This is why you cannot see with your ears or smell with your eyes.

Some receptors in your ears respond to sounds. Others respond when you turn your head so you can keep your balance.

Receptors inside your nose respond to chemicals in the air.

Receptors in your tongue respond to liquids or substances dissolved in saliva.

Receptors in your skin respond to touch, pressure, temperature and pain.

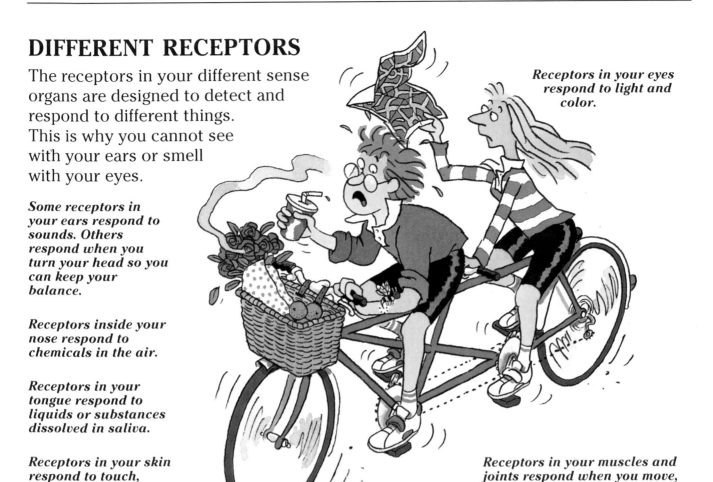

Receptors in your eyes respond to light and color.

Receptors in your muscles and joints respond when you move, so you know the position of parts of your body.

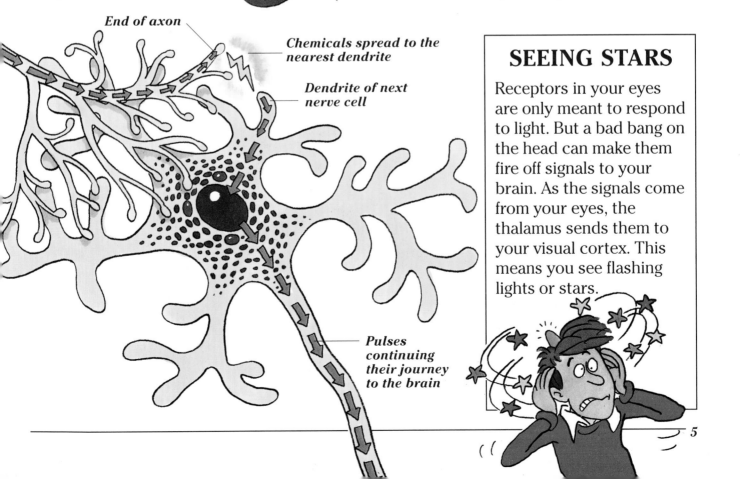

End of axon

Chemicals spread to the nearest dendrite

Dendrite of next nerve cell

Pulses continuing their journey to the brain

SEEING STARS

Receptors in your eyes are only meant to respond to light. But a bad bang on the head can make them fire off signals to your brain. As the signals come from your eyes, the thalamus sends them to your visual cortex. This means you see flashing lights or stars.

EYES & SEEING

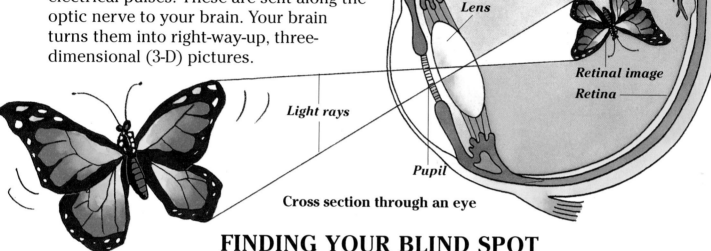

Your eyes are your window on the world. Light rays enter your eye through a tiny hole called the pupil. An upside-down, two-dimensional (flat) image of what's around you is projected onto a screen at the back of your eye called the retina. Receptors on the retina, called rods and cones, change this picture into electrical pulses. These are sent along the optic nerve to your brain. Your brain turns them into right-way-up, three-dimensional (3-D) pictures.

Optic nerve

Blood vessels

Lens

Retinal image

Retina

Light rays

Pupil

Cross section through an eye

FINDING YOUR BLIND SPOT

There are no rods or cones on the tiny spot where the optic nerve leaves the eye. This is called your blind spot. If an image falls exactly on your blind spot, you can't see it. You don't usually notice your blind spot because images usually fall on other parts of your retina too, and your brain just fills in the gap.

Line up the square man with your left eye. Close your right eye. Move the book slowly **away from you. When the book is about 30cm (1ft) away, the round man disappears.**

GETTING THINGS IN FOCUS

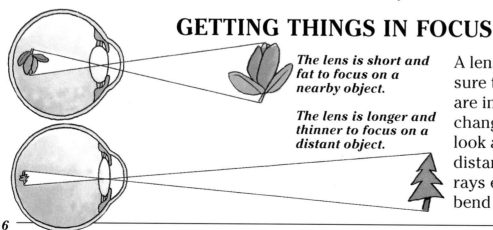

The lens is short and fat to focus on a nearby object.

The lens is longer and thinner to focus on a distant object.

A lens in your eye makes sure the objects you look at are in focus (not blurry). It changes shape when you look at things at different distances. This makes the rays entering your eye bend by different amounts.

WHY HAVE TWO EYES?

Hold a finger up about 25cm (10in) from your nose. Then focus on an object in the distance behind it. Shut each eye alternately, and watch your finger jump from side to side.

This happens because each eye sees your finger from a slightly different angle. Your brain joins the two images to help you see in 3-D. This is called binocular vision.

A RAINBOW WORLD

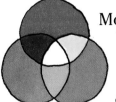

Most colors can be made by mixing the three basic colors of light: red, blue and green.

You can 'mix' colors in your eye in the same way. You have three types of cones on your retina: red, blue and green. Each type responds a different amount depending on what color you are looking at.

Ooohh, look! A bunch of grapes.

If you are looking at purple grapes, the blue and red cones respond more strongly than the green cones.

COLOR-BLINDNESS

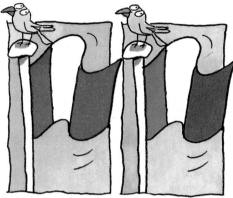

Normal color vision   *Colorblind vision*

Colorblind people can't tell the difference between red and green, because their red or green cones do not work properly.

They learn to call grass green, for example, just because other people do. Occasionally, people have normal vision in one eye, but are colorblind in the other one.

SEEING IN THE DARK

Cones don't work very well in dim light, so this is when you use your rods to see. Rods can't detect color, which is why it is hard to make out colors at night. But even rods need some light to work. They are helped by your pupils, which grow bigger in the dark. This is to let in as much light as possible.

While you are out in bright sunlight, you use your cones to see. Your rods don't work.

If you suddenly walk into a dark place, you can hardly see anything at first.

Your pupils soon enlarge, so more light enters your eyes. Your rods start working.

You may not like what you see lurking in the darkness!

For a link to a website where you can explore an online exhibit and find out how your mind sees color, go to **www.usborne-quicklinks.com**

MORE THAN MEETS THE EYE

A green tennis ball always looks like a green tennis ball, whether it's flying through the air in sunlight, or in the corner of a dark cupboard. This is because your brain uses four 'constancy mechanisms': size, brightness, color and shape. This means that you can recognize the things you look at, even though their image on your retina can be completely different in different situations.

SIZE

Two things that are the same size will project retinal images* of different sizes if one is farther away than the other. But your brain knows they are the same size.

*See picture of eye on page 6.

Your brain knows these ice cream cones are the same size, although their retinal images are different.

SHAPE

Shape constancy means that your brain tells you an object is the shape it would be if you were looking at it from straight on, even when you look at it from a different angle. So you know a door is a rectangle, even if the image on your retina is not rectangular at all.

BRIGHTNESS

Light things are brighter than dull things. But a light thing in a dim room can actually be duller than a dull thing in bright sunlight. But your brain still sees the thing as light, because it compares it to other duller things in the room.

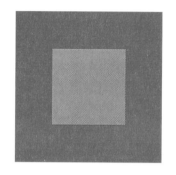

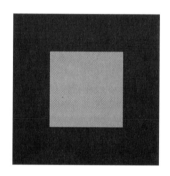

Because your brain compares things to their surroundings, this can lead to illusions. These gray squares are identical, but they don't look like it. The lighter the background, the darker the gray squares appear.

COLOR

Color constancy means a green apple still looks green, even if you are looking at it through red glasses. This is because it is still greener than everything else around it.

Perhaps I'll have a red apple after all!

HOW YOU SEE IN 3-D

Your brain is very good at figuring out how far away things are. It uses visual signals, called cues, in the retinal image to determine depth. This, along with binocular vision, gives you a 3-D picture of what you see.

Like a retinal image, this picture has cues to help you see it in 3-D.

Your brain interprets arrow-shaped lines as corners.

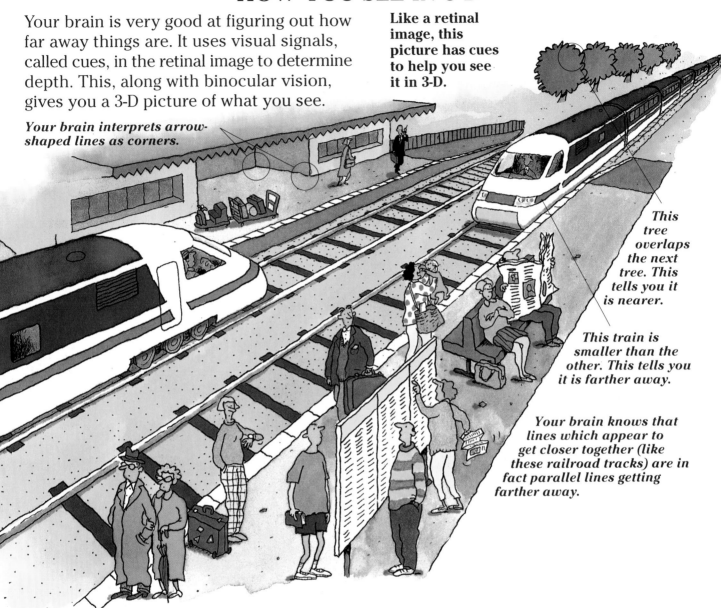

This tree overlaps the next tree. This tells you it is nearer.

This train is smaller than the other. This tells you it is farther away.

Your brain knows that lines which appear to get closer together (like these railroad tracks) are in fact parallel lines getting farther away.

SEEING WHAT YOU WANT TO SEE

Often what you see depends on what you are expecting to see, or what you want to see. For example, if you are hungry, you might catch a fleeting glimpse of a red ball and think it is a tomato. Or, if a familiar word is misspelled, you may not notice. This is because your brian has just assumed it is right. (Did you spot the deliberate mistake in this paragraph?)

The things around the object you look at also affect the way your brain analyzes it.

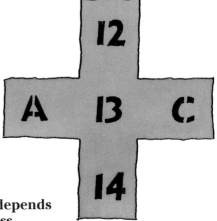

How you see the middle symbol depends on which way you look at the cross.

EARS & HEARING

If you drop a pebble into the middle of a pond, waves or ripples travel outward to the edges of the water. Sounds make the same kind of waves in the air, but of course you can't see sound waves. When sound waves travel into your ear, you can hear them.

This is the inside of your ear. It is divided into three parts:

| | Outer ear | | Middle ear | | Inner ear |

Malleus

Incus

Stapes

Cochlea: spiral-shaped tube

7

6

5

4

3

2

1

Auditory nerve to the brain

Ear drum: hole covered with a tight membrane (a thin skin)

Oval window: small hole covered by a membrane

The pinna: the part of your ear you can see. It helps to direct sound waves into the middle ear.

❶ Sound waves travel through the outer ear to the middle ear.

❷ The ear drum vibrates as the sound waves strike it.

❸ These vibrations pass along three tiny bones, the malleus, incus and stapes, to the oval window.

❹ From the oval window, the vibrations are carried along a membrane (a very thin skin) which divides the cochlea lengthways.

❺ The vibrating membrane stimulates tiny hairs in the cochlea. These hairs are receptor cells.

❻ The receptor hair cells convert the vibrations into electrical pulses, which pass along the auditory nerve to the brain.

❼ Your brain interprets electrical pulses as sounds, so you can hear.

AMPLITUDE AND PITCH

Sounds have different amplitude and pitch. Amplitude is another word for loudness. Pitch is how high or low a sound is. As a sound travels, its amplitude gets smaller. So the farther you are away from the source of a sound, the quieter it is.

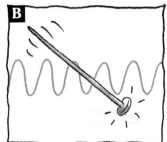

Sounds of different amplitudes make waves of different heights. Sound A is louder than B.

Sounds of different pitch have different frequencies. Frequency is the number of waves passing a given point in one second. Sound C is higher than D.

A violin, piano and saxophone all playing the same note at the same loudness don't all sound the same. This is because the sounds they produce have higher but quieter notes mixed in. These are called harmonics. Harmonics give an instrument its own individual sound.

DECIBELS

Loudness is measured in decibels (dB). The softest sound anyone can hear is 0dB.

0dB - Falling snow

30dB - A soft whisper

50dB - Quiet talk

70dB - Television

100dB - Subway train entering a station

110dB - Chain saw

120dB - Loud rock music

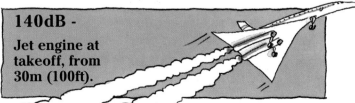

140dB - Jet engine at takeoff, from 30m (100ft).

11

BLINDNESS & DEAFNESS

Blindness and deafness can be severe handicaps because people use their eyes and ears more than any of their other senses. Nearly everything in our world is geared up for sighted and hearing people. Imagine trying to go shopping if you couldn't see or hear.

BLINDNESS

Severe damage to any part of the eye can cause blindness. Some people are born blind; others become blind because of disease or an accident.

Very few people can see nothing at all. These pictures show what a fruit stall looks like to people with different kinds of blindness.

Macular degeneration – damages the spot on the retina which lets you see best. A big blindspot develops.

Severe glaucoma – a disease of the eye which damages nerve cells. Can lead to "tunnel vision".

Diabetic retinopathy – damage to the retina, caused by diabetes. Sight becomes patchy and blurred.

Cataracts – make the lens go cloudy. Can happen when people get older, or because of injury to the eye.

There are no cures for most types of blindness, but cataracts can be cured by a simple operation. Sadly, in many countries, there is not enough money to perform the operation on everyone who needs it.

DEAFNESS

There are lots of causes of hearing problems. Some lead to only a small amount of deafness, but others can leave you totally deaf.

Some babies are born with hearing problems. Sometimes an illness such as meningitis can make you go deaf. As people get older, often their ears just stop working so well. Loud noises can also damage ears and cause deafness.

Ear protectors can prevent deafness.

HEARING AIDS

Many people who find it hard to hear wear hearing aids. These make sounds louder.

Hearing aids are made up of these basic parts:

Microphone – receives sound waves and turns them into electrical signals.

Amplifier – increases the strength of the electrical signal.

Earphone – converts electrical signals from the amplifier back into sound waves.

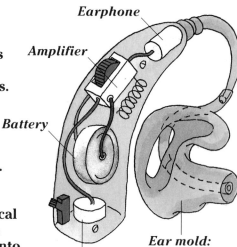

Earphone

Amplifier

Battery

Microphone

Ear mold: fits in ear

LIP READING

In a noisy place, hearing aids make everything louder so wearers often can't hear their own conversations. So, for many deaf people, lip reading is easier. Lip readers figure out what people are saying by looking at their lips, tongue and neck muscles. But even the best lip readers read only about half of the words spoken. They have to guess the rest.

Back to the light   **Hand on mouth**   **Beard over lips**

The things above make it hard for people to lip read.

SIGN LANGUAGES

People with serious hearing problems often use sign languages to talk to each other. Some sign languages use one hand gesture for each letter of the alphabet. Others use gestures, signs and facial expressions to express whole words, phrases and emotions. These sign languages are often incredibly complex, and have their own grammar and vocabulary.

"Your"

"name"

"what?"

This boy is asking "What is your name?", in British Sign Language (BSL). Try to answer using this alphabet sign language.

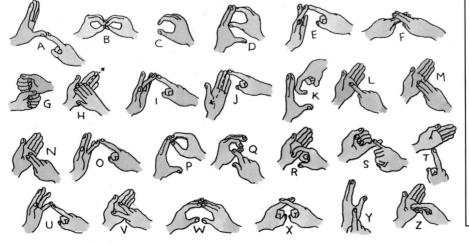

'P' OR 'B'?

People who are born deaf speak differently from hearing people. This is because they have never heard speech. Most of us learn to speak by imitating what we hear. A deaf person learns to imitate a sound or word by how it looks and feels.

**1. Look in a mirror and say 'p'. Now say 'b'.
Your lips moved in the same way for both sounds.**

2. Now say them again, but put your hand in front of your mouth. Can you feel the difference in the amount of air escaping?

This is how a deaf child learns to speak.

TASTE & SMELL

Y ou eat and drink because you need energy to live, and energy comes from food. But it would be really boring if your food had no taste or smell. Your receptors allow you to recognize a whole range of tastes, from chocolate to chili con carne.

TONGUE-TASTIC

Scientists think that all flavors are made up of four basic tastes: sweet, salty, sour and bitter. The things you eat are a mixture of these tastes. So, for example, oranges are sweet and sour, grapefruits less sweet and more sour, and chips are salty and a bit sweet.

Receptors on your tongue respond to chemicals in your food dissolved in saliva. Different parts of your tongue respond to each of the four basic tastes.

The picture above shows which parts of the tongue respond to which tastes.

Section of tongue

Your tongue contains hundreds of small bumps.

Each bump is surrounded by a small trench, which traps saliva.

Taste receptors lie in these trenches.

YUM OR YUK

The main purpose of your sense of taste is to tell you whether something is safe to eat. Dirt, muddy water and most poisonous plants taste horrid. So your immediate reaction is to spit them out. Most foods that are good for us don't taste nasty.

SWEET TOOTH

Many of us have a sweet tooth. This is because thousands of years ago, sweet things were extremely rare. But they were also extremely important, as they gave people a much needed energy boost.

So our ancestors developed a "taste" for sweet things, to make sure they would eat them whenever they found them.

For a link to a website where you can find out why orange juice tastes bad after you brush your teeth and then try an experiment using your taste buds, go to **www.usborne-quicklinks.com**

SUGAR AND SPICE

If you find it hard to believe that all the flavors of all the different foods come from only four tastes, you'd be right. This is because flavors aren't only made up of tastes, but also of smells.

You use these parts of your body to smell.

Part of brain which analyzes smell

Smell receptors

The inside of your nose is linked to your mouth, so you can smell food which is inside your mouth.

This is why, if your nose is blocked up with a really bad cold, you can feel as if you are eating cotton or cardboard.

The difference between taste and smell is that taste receptors respond to dissolved chemicals, while smell receptors respond to chemicals in the air.

Scientists don't understand exactly how smell receptors work. But, like tastes, they think there are probably only four basic smells: fragrant (like roses), fresh (like pine), spicy (like cinnamon) and putrid (like rotten eggs).

THE SMELLY T-SHIRT TEST

In order to test people's sense of smell, a group of men and women were asked to wear the same T-shirt for 24 hours without washing. The T-shirts were then sealed in plastic bags. Each person was asked to take a sniff of three bags: one containing their own T-shirt, and two belonging to strangers – one man's and one woman's. About 75% of people could identify their own T-shirt and tell the difference between the man's and the woman's T-shirts.

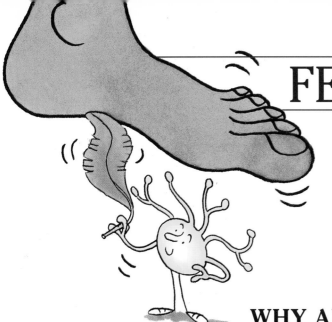

FEELING TOUCHY

The skin is not just a bag to keep your body parts in – it's the biggest sense organ in your body. It contains millions of receptors which respond to touch, pain, pressure and heat and cold. These receptors send electrical signals to your brain and give you a mass of information about what different things feel like.

WHY ARE FEET TICKLISH?

If you want to make a ticklish person squirm, tickle their feet. The soles of the feet are very sensitive to light touch, which makes them more ticklish than most other parts of your body.

In the same way that feet are more sensitive to light touch, other parts of your body are more sensitive to other qualities. Some respond most to heat, some to cold, and others to pain. Exactly what your sense of touch tells you about a particular thing depends upon the number and type of receptors in the part of the skin that touches it.

This diagram shows the main receptors found in different parts of your skin.

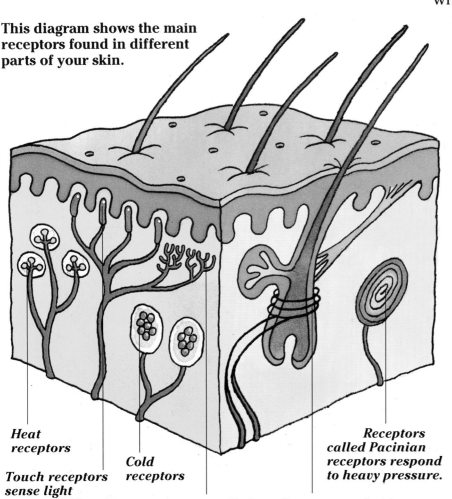

Heat receptors

Touch receptors sense light pressure. They tell you about the texture of things.

Cold receptors

Receptors called free nerve endings react to pain.

Receptors called Pacinian receptors respond to heavy pressure.

Receptors at hair roots detect pressure through the movement of the hair.

READING WITH FINGERS

Blind people use their sense of touch to read a code called Braille, made from raised dots.

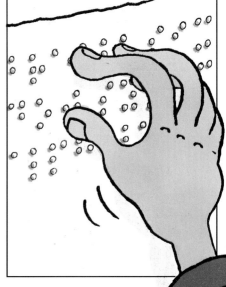

For a link to a website where you can learn the alphabet in Braille, see your name in Braille and solve some Braille riddles, go to www.usborne-quicklinks.com

WHAT'S THE POINT?

Your fingertips contain more touch receptors than any other part of your body. This makes them very sensitive. Try this experiment to feel the difference between the sensitivity of your fingertip and the back of your leg.

Place the points of a divider 2mm apart.

Touch a fingertip lightly. You should feel two separate points.

Now touch the back of your leg. It feels like just one point.

HOT AND COLD

Your skin contains heat and cold receptors. They both respond most strongly when they are first activated. If you are outside sunbathing on a hot day, and then go indoors, it feels very cold at first. But, after a while, it starts to feel normal, as your cold receptors adapt to the new situation.

BARELY THERE

You hardly notice the clothes you are wearing, even though they are touching you all the time. This is because when you are in contact with the same thing for some time, your touch receptors stop responding as they get used to it. So even clothes with annoying, itchy labels will start to feel less itchy after a while.

FEEL THE PRESSURE

When you use a pencil to write with, the pencil acts as an extension of your finger. Your pressure receptors respond to the object you touch with the pencil, even though your skin is not touching it directly. Try using a stick to touch different kinds of surfaces. Can you feel the difference?

TESTING THE WATER

Do this experiment and feel your temperature receptors in action.

1. Prepare three bowls, one filled with cold water, one with warm water, and the third with hot water (not *too* hot).

2. Put your right foot in hot water and your left foot in cold water.

3. Then plunge both feet into the bowl of warm water.

4. Your right foot feels cold in the warm bowl, but your left foot feels hot.

This experiment works because cold receptors in the right foot are activated for the first time, so they respond more strongly than the heat receptors. But the opposite happens in your left foot, where the heat receptors respond more strongly than the cold receptors.

A PAINFUL SUBJECT

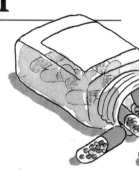

If someone punched you on the nose, or if you stood on broken glass, you would feel pain. Although pain is not very nice, it's very important. It tells you that your body is in danger. You feel pain when receptors respond to something which is causing you damage. They send urgent messages to your brain. You can then do something to try to stop the pain.

REFLEX ACTIONS

Sometimes, you move away from a thing that is hurting you before you actually feel the pain and know what you are doing. This is called a reflex action.

Reflex actions happen when messages from pain receptors are sent to the spinal cord, not the brain. You don't become aware of the pain, or the movement away from it, until messages are sent from the spinal cord to the brain telling it what has been happening.

This picture shows what happens during a reflex action.

Pain signals are sent from hand to spinal cord.

Nerve cell in spine

Small section of spinal cord

Nerve cells carry instructions to muscles to move hand.

REFERRED PAIN

If someone damages an organ in their body, they may feel pain somewhere else completely. This is called referred pain.

Referred pain happens because pain receptors from different areas of your body meet at the same place in the spinal cord. The brain confuses where the messages are coming from.

This picture shows the areas where you can feel referred pain when certain organs are damaged.

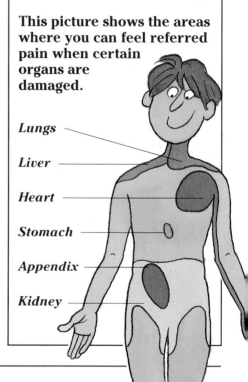

Lungs

Liver

Heart

Stomach

Appendix

Kidney

For a link to a website where you can test your reflexes, go to
www.usborne-quicklinks.com

CONTROLLING AND RELIEVING PAIN

There are lots of different ways of controlling pain. One way is by taking painkilling drugs.

Painkillers don't cure illnesses and injuries, but they are chemicals which stop you from feeling pain. One of the strongest painkillers is morphine. It is used to help control very severe pain.

Your brain also produces its own painkillers, called endorphins. These work in the same way as morphine does. They are usually released after pain is first felt, but they often stop working once the immediate crisis is over.

Endorphins mean that even people who are very badly wounded often don't feel pain from their wounds until later. This may give them the time to get help.

A man bitten by a lion feels pain.

But endorphins reduce the pain, enabling him to crawl to safety.

Soothing music can help people block out pain.

As well as producing endorphins, scientists think your brain can also block pain signals coming from the spinal cord. No one understands exactly how this works.

People seem to be able to develop their own ways of relieving pain. This might be by singing, listening to music, deep breathing, or tightly holding or biting something. Scientists can't explain why these things help.

MIND OVER MATTER

How much pain people feel is not only to do with the strength of the signals from pain receptors. Other things, such as a person's culture and attitude of mind, also have a big effect. In some Eastern religions, people take part in rituals which would be unbearably painful to Westerners. But they don't seem to feel any pain.

This man looks quite relaxed on his bed of nails.

TRICKY POSITIONS

Your brain receives messages from receptors in muscles all over your body. They tell your brain the position of all your limbs and joints. Your brain analyzes the information it is sent and uses it to coordinate all your movements. This means you can cross your legs and scratch your nose at the same time without falling over.

MOVING MUSCLES

You move parts of your body using pairs of muscles. These are attached to your bones by tough bands called tendons. By monitoring muscles and tendons, your brain works out what you are doing with your arms and legs.

These pictures show how a pair of muscles moves your arm.

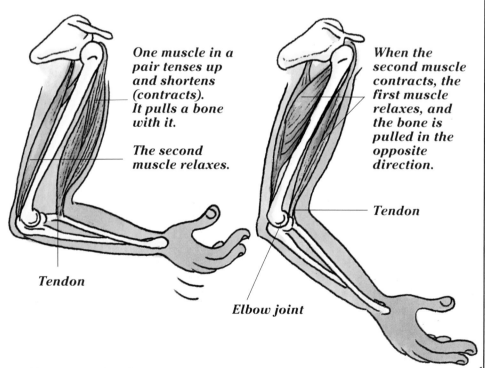

One muscle in a pair tenses up and shortens (contracts). It pulls a bone with it.

The second muscle relaxes.

Tendon

When the second muscle contracts, the first muscle relaxes, and the bone is pulled in the opposite direction.

Tendon

Elbow joint

Deep inside these muscles and tendons are receptors. These send messages to your brain about the length of the muscle and the tension on the tendons. Using this information, your brain can figure out whether an arm or leg is bent or straight.

MUSCLE MONITOR

Another way your brain knows the position of some parts of your body is by monitoring its own commands. It keeps track of instructions that have been sent to certain muscles.

You use this monitoring system for seeing. Your eye muscles move constantly. So the image on your retina is always jumping around. But you don't see it like this.

This is because your brain takes into account its commands to your eye muscles when interpreting the image on your retina.

KEEP YOUR HEAD

Inside your inner ear you have a special system, called the vestibular system. It helps you keep your balance and tells you which direction you are moving in.

The vestibular system

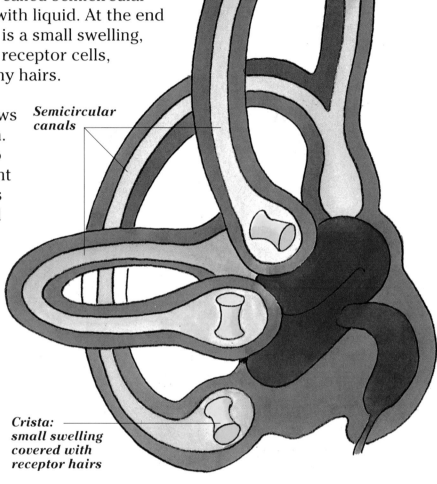

The vestibular system is made up of three tunnels, called semicircular canals, filled with liquid. At the end of each canal is a small swelling, covered with receptor cells, shaped like tiny hairs.

Semicircular canals

When you move, the liquid flows over the hairs and bends them. This bending is converted into electrical signals which are sent to the brain. Your brain figures out which way up you are, and where you are going, by analyzing these signals.

In a car, your eyes tell your brain you are moving, but your vestibular system says you are still. This can make you car sick.

Crista: small swelling covered with receptor hairs

DIZZY SPELLS

Have you ever spun around in a circle so that when you stop you're so dizzy you fall over in a heap on the floor? This happens because the liquid in your semi-circular canals keeps on spinning after your body has stopped. The same thing happens with water in a glass.

Rotate a glass of water in your hand. The water in the glass will continue swirling after you have stopped moving the glass.

BRAIN BLINDNESS

There are several parts of your brain which deal with sight. If any of them is damaged, very strange things can happen to the way you see the outside world. Studying people with this kind of brain damage is very important to doctors. It can help them understand which part of the brain does what, when interpreting images on your retina.

FAMILIAR FACES?

People are better at recognizing faces than anything else. If you were shown 50 photos of faces one day, and then the same 50, plus 50 new ones the next day, you could tell the new from the old very easily.

But if you were to damage a tiny area on the right-hand side of your brain, you wouldn't be able to recognize any faces at all – not even your own.

The strange thing is that it is only faces that cause these difficulties. People with this problem can recognize someone by their clothes, voice or even handwriting. This makes scientists think there may be one part of the brain that is specially designed to recognize faces.

WHAT IS IT?

Brain damage to a similar area of the brain (on either the right or left side) can leave people being able to see objects without understanding what they are. Once they can touch something, they can identify it easily.

Someone brain damaged in this way looked at a mug and described it as a cylinder with a loop attached to one side. She didn't know what it was until she picked it up.

I think it's stopped!

An ex-doctor described a stethoscope as a long cord with a round thing at one end and two rigid cords attached at the other. The only thing he thought it could be was a watch.

LEFT BLINDNESS

 Damage to an area at the back of the right-hand side of the brain can stop people from 'seeing' anything on their left-hand side, even though their eyes are working perfectly. When asked to copy a drawing, these people will draw the right-hand side of the picture accurately, but leave out the left-hand side altogether. They cannot even imagine a complete scene in their mind.

When asked to divide a horizontal line in half, a woman with left blindness drew a line near the right end of the line.

An Italian man was asked to pretend he was standing at one end of a famous square in Milan and to describe what he could see in front of him. He described exactly the right-hand half of the square, but didn't mention the left.

BLIND SIGHT

 Each receptor in your retina sends messages to one particular point on your visual cortex (see page 4). If part of the visual cortex is damaged, the part of the retina which sends messages to that part of the cortex seems not to work. The person develops a big blind spot. If an object is positioned so it falls on this blind spot, that person will say they can't see it. The pictures below show an experiment carried out on hundreds of people with this brain damage. It proves that the objects ARE seen, but in a part of the brain the patients aren't aware of.

A shape is held up so its image falls on the patient's blind spot.

The patient claims not to be able to see it.

When asked to guess the shape, nearly all patients guess right.

ANIMAL SENSES

We think that we perceive the world as it really is. In fact, our senses give us a limited view of it. Many animals have sense organs that are very different from ours. This means that their experience of the world around them is different. They may be able to hear sounds too high for human ears, or smell scents that we wouldn't catch a whiff of.

PROUD AS A PEACOCK

When a peacock wants to attract a mate, it shows off its bright feathers. Since this display would be wasted on a colorblind peahen, we can guess from this that they can see in color.

Me..? Vain..?

Most animals, however, don't have color vision. This is because they are descended from animals which hunted at night. Because colors can't be seen in the dark, color vision would have been useless.

FOLLOW THE SCENT

Many animals that hunt for food use their sense of smell to track down their prey. Sharks can smell even a tiny drop of blood in the ocean.

Ouch! Hope there are no sharks about!

Some dogs are one million times more sensitive to smells than we are. The police use specially trained dogs to help them hunt for missing people and to search for bombs, using their sense of smell. In 1925, a Doberman Pinscher tracked two thieves 160km (100 miles) across the desert in South Africa just by following their scent.

From smelling a piece of clothing, dogs can track down the person it belongs to.

SNIFF... SNIFF...

SWAT THE FLY

If you've ever tried to swat a fly, you'll know how hard it is, even if you creep up on one from behind. There are two reasons for this. Flies, like all insects, receive visual information very quickly. This means they can react to things very fast. Flies also have large, curved eyes, giving them good all-around vision. So they can spot you coming from any direction.

But although they can avoid the swat, insects can't actually see very well. Their eyes are made up of lots of minute lenses, so they see the world as made up of hundreds of tiny dots.

A fly's eye magnified more than 100 times

HEAT WAVE

A rattlesnake can track down prey by the heat it gives off. On either side of the snake's head is a pit containing heat receptors. These detect any increase in temperature in its surroundings, sensing the body heat of the snake's next victim.

BLIND AS A BAT

Bats have poor eyesight, but very good hearing. They can hear sounds too high for human ears to detect. Their sense of hearing helps them hunt for food and find their way in the dark.

Bats make high-pitched squeaks and then wait for echoes to bounce back off the objects in their path. From the echoes, they can tell the size and position of objects around them. This is called echo location.

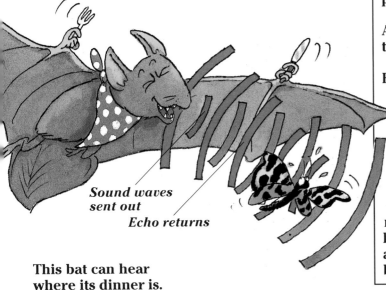

Sound waves sent out

Echo returns

This bat can hear where its dinner is.

A SENSE OF DIRECTION

Birds that migrate to warmer places in winter have to travel thousands of miles. Scientists have discovered that they have a kind of internal "clock", which helps them do this. It is like an extra sense.

It allows them to use the Sun as a compass. Without it, the Sun would be no use as a guide, because it changes position throughout the day. But if you know it's six in the morning, you know the Sun is in the East, so you can use it to work out every other direction.

Migrating birds fly over thousands of miles. Many return to exactly the same spot year after year.

FASCINATING FACTS

A sperm whale can stun or even kill its prey by making loud noises.

A lizard called the tuatura has a third eye on top of its brain.

Blue whales have eyes as big as footballs.

Grasshoppers' ears are in their knees.

The African elephant has the biggest nose of any mammal. A large male's trunk is about 2.5m (8ft) from base to tip.

For a link to a website where you can find out lots more information about animal senses and hear a whale's song, go to **www.usborne-quicklinks.com**

LEARNING TO SENSE

When a baby is born, most of its senses organs are fully formed. But babies can't sense things in the way older children and adults can. This is because a baby's brain has not yet developed enough to analyze the messages it receives from its senses.

Scientists think that babies' senses are programmed to develop in a certain way, but that other things can affect them. How and where a baby is brought up, and what it is taught, can make a difference to how its senses work.

BLURRY FACES

Newborn babies' eyes still have some growing to do before they are perfectly formed. So they can't see as well as you.

This is what a face looks like to a newborn baby.

By 6 months, it can see as well as an adult.

TOWN AND COUNTRY

Comparing children who live in town and the country, it is possible to see differences in how their senses work because of where they live. For example, a city child may judge how fast a car is traveling, through sight, sound and touch (the feel of wind as a car whizzes past). This will help him cross a busy road. A child from a farm may not be able do this so easily. But she may be able to tell a sheep apart from its flock.

For a link to a website where you can listen to an unusual version of a well-known story, go to www.usborne-quicklinks.com

LEARNING TO HEAR

As they get older, babies' brains learn only to tune into sounds which are familiar. This means they lose the ability to say and hear sounds they don't hear very often. This is why, for example, Japanese children can't hear or say the difference between l and r sounds. In Japanese there is only one sound for these, somewhere in between the two.

At 6 months, all babies, from all over the world, babble the same sounds.

But by 12 months or so, babies only babble the sounds they hear in their own language.

DOUBLE DUTCH

When foreigners talk, it can sound as if they are talking really quickly. It's even hard to tell where one word ends and another begins. They are probably speaking no faster than you do, but your brain has not learned to 'hear' their language.

PERFECT SENSE

If you use a particular sense a lot for a particular job, your brain gets better at interpreting the information it receives.

Expert wine tasters can tell if a wine is from Italy, U.S.A., Australia, or a particular region of France, which variety of grapes were used to make it, and even what year it was made.

Perfume companies employ people with a trained sense of smell to test out their perfumes for them.

Bird watchers can identify birds which, to the untrained eye, just look like brown blobs.

JUST AN ILLUSION?

In general your senses do a pretty good job of telling you about the world around you. But not always. Sometimes they can give you false information. These are called illusions. Most illusions occur because of the way your senses work. This means scientists can get useful information about your senses by studying illusions.

ELECTRICAL FAULTS

Your receptors fire off more electrical pulses when they are first activated. But once they are used to a situation, they fire off fewer. Many illusions, such as the one below, happen because of this.

Stare at this flower for 30 seconds.

Now look at a sheet of white paper, and blink a few times.

The image of a flower should appear, but with red petals.

This happens because white has red and green light in it. When you look at the white paper, your red receptors are responding for the first time, so they fire off lots of pulses. Your green receptors have already been responding, so they fire off fewer. This makes you see red petals.

SOUND ILLUSION

When a police car speeds past you, the pitch of the siren suddenly changes from high to low, although the noise of the siren is actually quite regular. This happens because the closer together sound waves are, the higher the pitch of the sound.

The sound waves coming from the police car bunch up together as the car moves toward you, so the siren sounds higher than it really is. As the car moves away, the waves behind it appear to spread out. This makes the sound seem lower.

TOUCH ILLUSION

Your sense of touch is fooled in this experiment because you are using your fingers in a way your brain is not used to.

1. Take a small round lid or a large coin, more than 2.5cm (1in) across.

2. Hold it between your left thumb and forefinger.

3. Close your eyes and turn the lid with the right thumb and forefinger.

You should get the feeling that a perfectly round object is oval-shaped.

This illusion works better for some people than others. The larger the object and the faster you turn it, the stronger the illusion should be.

PERSPECTIVE ILLUSIONS

Your brain turns the flat images on your retina into three-dimensional scenes. Many visual illusions happen when your brain tries to do the same thing to flat pictures on a page.

Try these quiz questions and see how your brain can trick you. Don't use a ruler to help you.

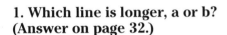

2. Which man in this picture is the tallest? (Answer on page 32.)

1. Which line is longer, a or b? (Answer on page 32.)

WHERE'S THE SQUARE?

Sometimes when you look at a pattern, regular shapes can appear distorted. Because the combination of shapes is unfamiliar, your brain doesn't know how to interpret the image.

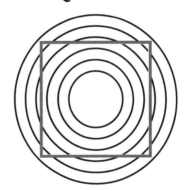

3. Which of the patterns contains a perfect square? (Answer on page 32.)

DUCK OR RABBIT?

Sometimes, something you look at can be one of two things. But there are not strong enough features for your brain to make its mind up which one is correct.

This picture can be either an old or a young woman.

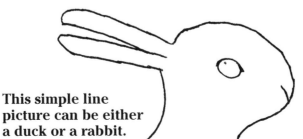

This simple line picture can be either a duck or a rabbit.

This is a vase or two faces in profile. Which did you see first?

SMART MACHINES

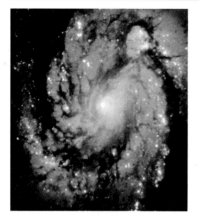

For hundreds of years, people have used equipment to help them see and hear things which they couldn't using only their own senses. Today, computers have been developed that not only improve our senses, but can also actually sense things for themselves.

The Hubble telescope allows human eyes to see millions of light years away. This is a spiral galaxy, about 50 million light years from Earth.

COMPUTER SENSES

Computers can sense things just as you can. But, instead of sense organs, they have input hardware. Input hardware converts information into a series of electrical signals, called binary code. Binary code can be analyzed by a computer's processor. This is like the brain of the computer.

A computer processor

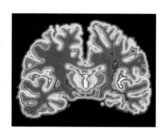

A brain cross-section

This picture shows how computers work in a similar way to your senses and brain.

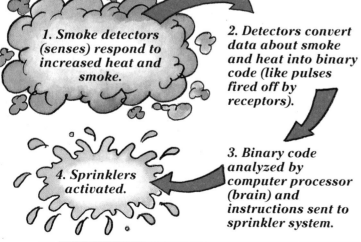

1. Smoke detectors (senses) respond to increased heat and smoke.

2. Detectors convert data about smoke and heat into binary code (like pulses fired off by receptors).

3. Binary code analyzed by computer processor (brain) and instructions sent to sprinkler system.

4. Sprinklers activated.

COMPUTER SIGHT

Scanners are the "eyes" of a computer. They can see images or printed text, and translate them into binary code. The computer reads the code and can recreate the image or text on screen.

X-ray scanners are used in hospitals to see inside the human body. If enough x-rays are taken, a computer can build up 3-D images of the inside of your body.

Ah, looks like 011010010!

Hand-held scanner

Although scanners can see things you can't, scientists have yet to make a computer that works as well as the brain. For example, computers are pretty bad at recognizing faces - a task which humans can perform at only a few months old.

TOUCH SENSITIVE

A touchscreen is a computer screen with a built-in system of wires which can feel touch. Touchscreens are often used in information centers. You can select options and give commands by pressing different areas on a screen.

VOICE RECOGNITION

Some computers can hear. They convert sound waves into electrical signals. But computers have as many problems with voices as they do with faces. No one has yet developed a computer which can easily follow instructions from people's voices. This is because people speak in so many different ways it would need a very complicated processor.

VIRTUAL REALITY SENSES

Computers can create worlds that don't exist, and make you believe you can see, hear and touch them. This is called virtual reality. In the virtual world, just by putting on some special equipment, you could land a plane (pilots train like this) or creep through a haunted house.

The girl in the picture is wearing a headset and data gloves. Sensors in the headset pick up head movements. They convert this information into signals which are sent to a computer. As her head moves, the computer changes the image on the headset's screens, and adjusts the sound. Sensors in her data gloves detect hand movements in the same way.

This girl is wearing special virtual reality gear.

The headset has two screens in front of each eye. 3-D scenes are projected onto these screens.

Data gloves

The headset also contains earphones with stereo sound.

QUIZ ANSWERS FROM P.29
1. They are both the same length.
2. They are all the same height.
3. All of them.

Acknowledgements
Cover: Nancy Kedersha/Science Photo Library; p.12: Isabelle Lilly, Photographer (with thanks to the RNIB); p.19: Corbis-Bettmann; p.24: David Scharf/Science Photo Library; p.26: Sue Atkinson, Photographer (with thanks to Charles York-Miller); p.29: Mary Evans Picture Library (After Boring, 1930); p.30: spiral galaxy - Space Telescope Science Institute/NASA/Science Photo Library; computer processor - Alfred Pasieka/Science Photo Library; brain cross section - Scott Camazine/Science Photo Library.